Suzuki

PIANO SCHOOL

Volume 7
New International Edition

© 1978, 1995, 2008, 2010 Dr. Shinichi Suzuki
Sole publisher for the entire world except Japan:
Summy-Birchard, Inc.
Exclusive print rights administered by
Alfred Music Publishing
All rights reserved.   Printed in USA.

Book alone:
ISBN-10: 0-7390-6001-5
ISBN-13: 978-0-7390-6001-8

Book & CD:
ISBN-10: 0-7390-5999-8
ISBN-13: 978-0-7390-5999-9

The Suzuki name, logo and wheel device
are trademarks of Dr. Shinichi Suzuki used
under exclusive license by Summy-Birchard, Inc.

Any duplication, adaptation or arrangement of the compositions
contained in this collection requires the written consent of the Publisher.
No part of this book may be photocopied or reproduced in any way without permission.
Unauthorized uses are an infringement of the U.S. Copyright Act and are punishable by law.

INTRODUCTION

This volume is part of the worldwide Suzuki Method of teaching. The companion recording should be used along with each volume.

For the parent: Credentials are essential for any Suzuki teacher you choose. We recommend that you ask your teacher for his or her credentials, especially relating to training in the Suzuki Method. The Suzuki Method experience should foster a positive relationship among teacher, parent and child. Choosing the right teacher is of the utmost importance.

For the teacher: To be an effective teacher ongoing study and education are essential. Each Regional Suzuki Association provides Teacher Training and Teacher Development for members. It is strongly recommended that all teachers be members of their regional or country associations.

To obtain more information about your Regional Suzuki Association, contact the International Suzuki Association: www.internationalsuzuki.org

This revised edition of the Suzuki Piano School was produced through the cooperative effort of the International Suzuki Piano Committee. Many markings for tempi and dynamics, for phrasings and articulations, and for fingerings and pedaling are editorial, especially in music written during the Baroque era. Alternate fingerings are given in parentheses.

INTRODUCTION

Ces matériaux appartiennent à la méthode Suzuki telle qu'elle est enseignée dans les différents pays du monde. Les enregistrements accompagnants doivent être utilisés en combinaison avec cette publication.

Pour les parents: Les qualifications sont essentielles dans le choix du professeur. Aussi nous vous recommandons de demander au professeur quels sont ses diplômes et notamment ceux qui ont trait à l'enseignement de la méthode Suzuki. L'apprentissage par la méthode Suzuki doit être une expérience positive, où il existe une relation épanouissante entre l'enfant, le parent et le professeur. Le choix du bon professeur est dès lors d'une importance cruciale.

Pour le professeur: Afin d'enseigner d'une manière efficace selon la pédagogie instrumentale Suzuki, une formation est exigée. Votre association Suzuki régionale ou nationale peut vous offrir une telle formation si vous en êtes membre. Les professeurs sont encouragés à adhérer à leur association Suzuki régionale ou nationale.

De plus amples informations concernant l'Association Suzuki dans votre région peuvent être obtenues sur le site de l'Association internationale de Suzuki: www.internationalsuzuki.org

L'édition revue du volume Suzuki pour piano a été réalisée grâce à la coopération du Comité international de Suzuki pour piano. La plupart des indications de rythme, de dynamique, de phrasé, d'articulation, de doigté et de pédales sont de l'éditeur, en particulier pour la musique écrite durant l'âge baroque. Des doigtés alternatifs sont suggérés entre parenthèses.

EINLEITUNG

Dieses Heft ist Teil der weltweit verbreiteten „Suzuki-Methode". Die dazugehörende Aufnahme sollte stets mit verwendet werden.

Für die Eltern: Jede(r) Suzuki-Lehrer(in) sollte eine entsprechende Ausbildung nachweisen können. Wir empfehlen Ihnen deshalb, Ihre Lehrperson nach ihrer Suzuki-Ausbildung zu fragen. Der Suzuki-Unterricht sollte eine gute Beziehung zwischen Eltern, Kind und Lehrperson fördern. Die Wahl des richtigen Lehrers bzw. der richtigen Lehrerin ist deswegen von höchster Bedeutung.

Für die Lehrer: Um erfolgreich unterrichten zu können, ist ständige Weiterbildung unabdingbar. Jede Nationale Suzuki-Gesellschaft bietet Möglichkeiten zur Aus- und Weiterbildung an. Es ist sehr zu empfehlen, dass alle Suzuki-Lehrer ihrer Nationalen Suzuki-Vereinigung angehören.

Für weitere Informationen: www.internationalsuzuki.org

Diese überarbeitete Ausgabe der Suzuki-Klavierschule entstand in gemeinschaftlicher Arbeit von Mitgliedern des Internationalen Suzuki-Klavier-Komitees. Viele Angaben zum Tempo und zur Dynamik, zur Phrasierung und zur Artikulation, Fingersätze und Pedalangaben stammen von den Herausgebern, insbesondere gilt dies für die Stücke aus dem Barockzeitalter. Alternative Fingersätze sind in Klammern angegeben.

INTRODUCCIÓN

Este material es parte del mundialmente conocido Método Suzuki de enseñanza. Las grabaciones complementarias deben de ser usadas con estas publicaciones.

Para los padres: Es importante que el profesor que escojan tenga certificados de estudios. Recomendamos que pidan al profesor que muestre dichos documentos, especialmente aquellos relacionados con el Método Suzuki. La experiencia de aprender con el Método Suzuki, debe ser única y positiva para los alumnos, en la que exista una maravillosa y estrecha relación entre el niño, el padre y el maestro. Por eso es de mayor importancia escoger al maestro adecuado.

Para el maestro: Para ser un maestro Suzuki de calidad, se requiere de una preparación intensa y constante. Las Asociaciones Suzuki de cada región proveen de dicha preparación a sus miembros. Es fuertemente recomendable que los profesores sean miembros de la asociación Suzuki de su país y de la asociación Suzuki de su región.

Con el objetivo de obtener más información acerca del Método Suzuki en su país, por favor contacten con la Internacional Suzuki Association: www.internationalsuzuki.org

Esta edición revisada de los libros para Piano del Método Suzuki fue realizada a través de un esfuerzo de cooperación del Comité Internacional de Piano Suzuki. Varias indicaciones de tempo, dinámica, fraseo, articulación, digitación y pedal son sugerencias editoriales, especialmente de la música escrita durante el periodo Barroco. Digitaciones alternativas se muestran entre paréntesis.

CONTENTS

	Track	Page

1. Sonata in A Major, K. 331 (300i), *Wolfgang Amadeus Mozart*
- Andante grazioso 1 4
- Minuetto and Trio 2 14
- Alla turca 3 18

2. Prelude & Fugue in D Major, BWV 850,
from *The Well-Tempered Clavier, Book 1,* *Johann Sebastian Bach*
- Prelude 4 23
- Fugue 5 26

3. Nocturne in C-sharp Minor, Op. posthumous, *Frédéric Chopin* 6 29

4. The Harmonious Blacksmith, from *Suite No. 5 in E Major,* *George F. Handel* 7 33

5. La fille aux cheveux de lin, from *Préludes, Book 1,* **L. 117:8,** *Claude Debussy* 8 38

6. Romanian Folk Dances, Sz. 56, *Béla Bartók*
- 1. Joc cu Bâtă 9 41
- 2. Brâul 10 43
- 3. Pe loc 11 44
- 4. Buciumeana 12 46
- 5. Poargă Românească 13 47
- 6. Măruntelul 14 49

Sonata in A Major
Sonate en la majeur
Sonate in A-dur
Sonata en la mayor

Wolfgang Amadeus Mozart (1756–1791)
K. 331 (300i)

(a) Although pedal will be used in the Theme, specific markings have not been indicated in the music. The exact pedal to be used will be determined by each individual performer depending upon the sound of the instrument and the acoustics of the room.

Bien qu'on se serve de la pédale dans le thème, on n'indique pas les pédales précises sur la partition. Il appartient donc à l'exécutant de choisir les pédales selon la sonorité de l'instrument et l'acoustique de la salle.

Obwohl im Thema Pedal verwendet wird, sind im Notentext keine Pedalisierungsangaben vermerkt. Der Pedalgebrauch sollte - abhängig vom Klang des Instruments und der Raumakustik - vom Spieler selbst festgelegt werden.

Aunque el pedal va a ser usado en el tema, no se han indicado marcas específicas en la música. El pedal exacto a utilizarse será determinado por cada ejecutante, dependiendo del sonido del instrumento y la acústica del salón.

(e) Half pedal may be used on Var. III.
On peut employer une demi-pédale dans la Variation III.

In Var. III kann Halbpedal benutzt werden.
En la Variación III se puede usar medio pedal.

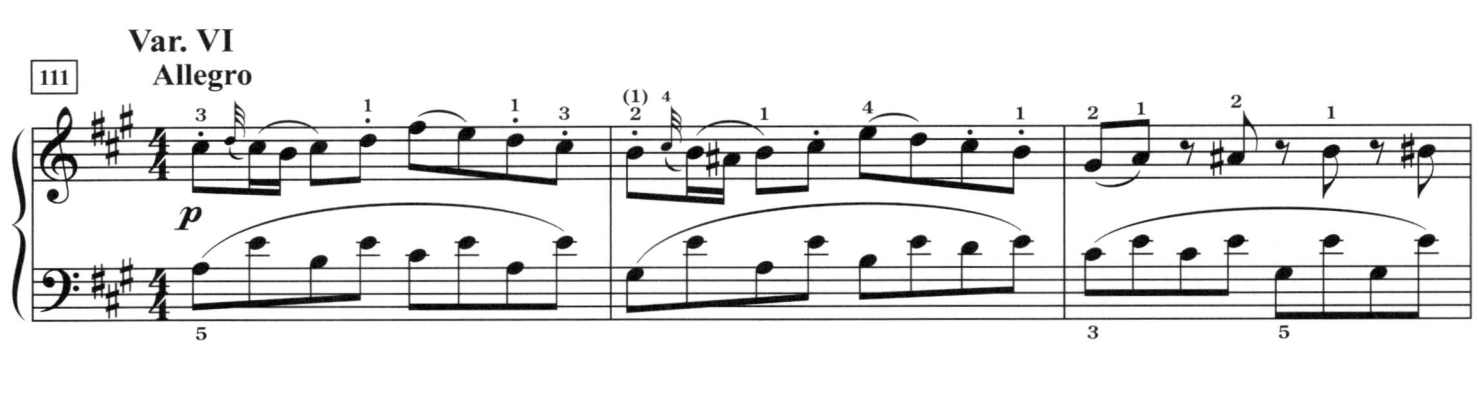
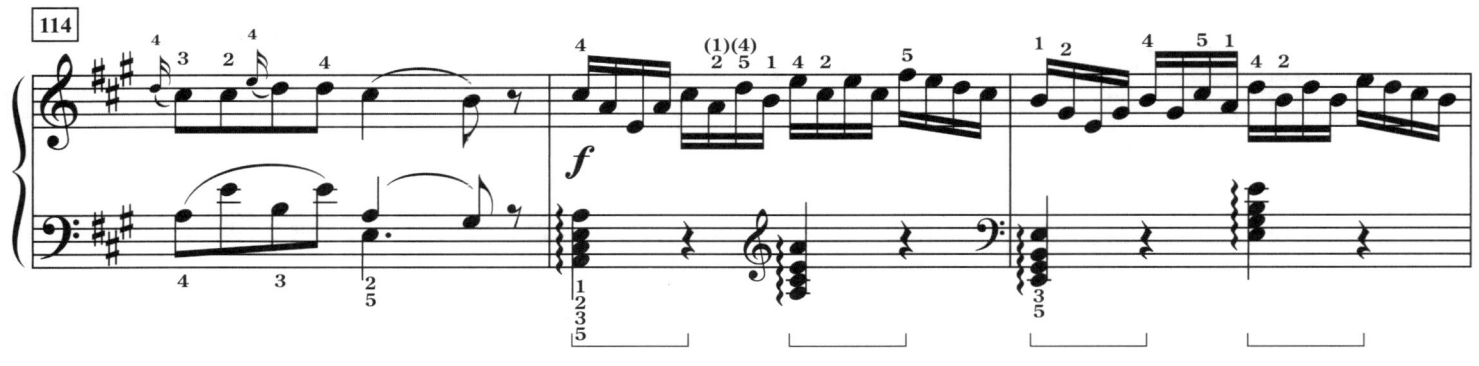
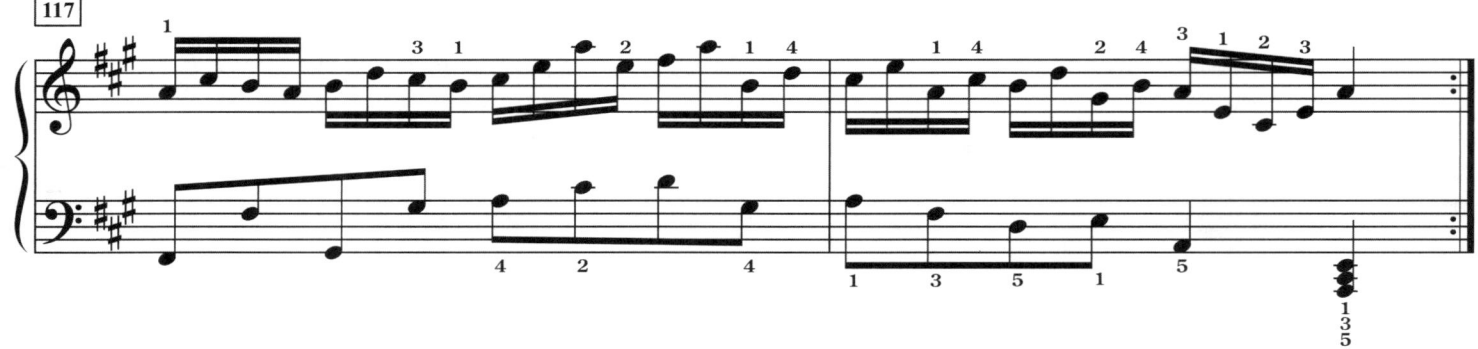

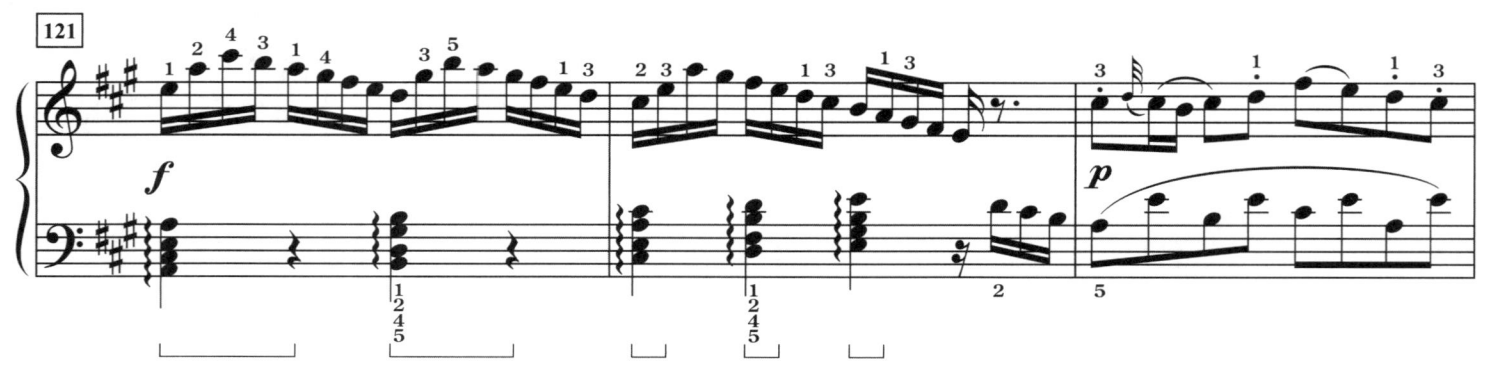

(f) Alternate fingering:
un autre doigté possible:
Alternativer Fingersatz:
Digitación alternativa:

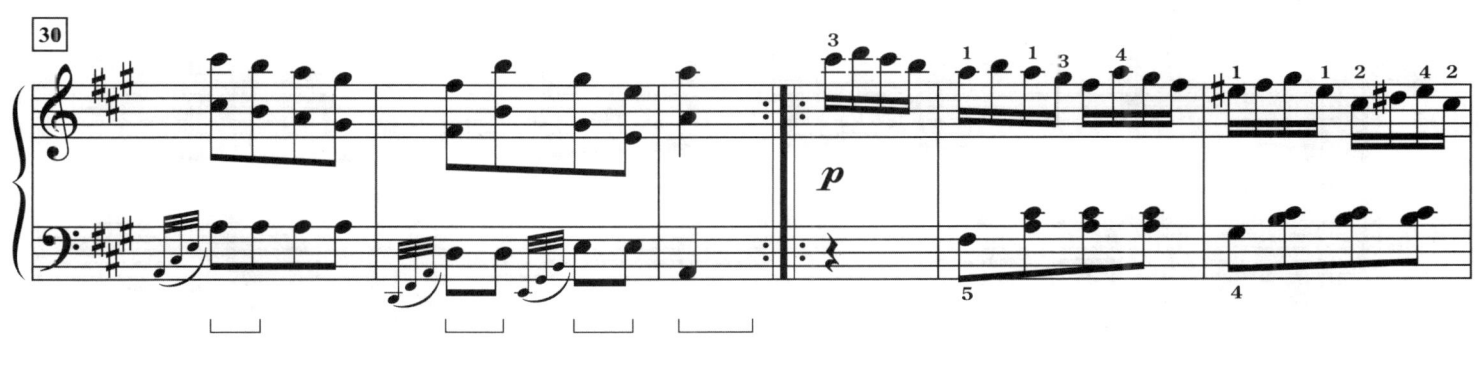

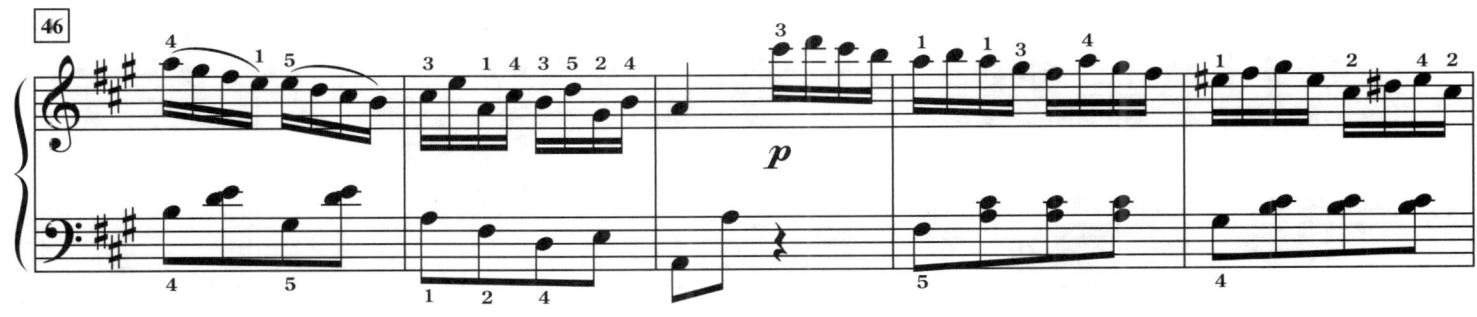
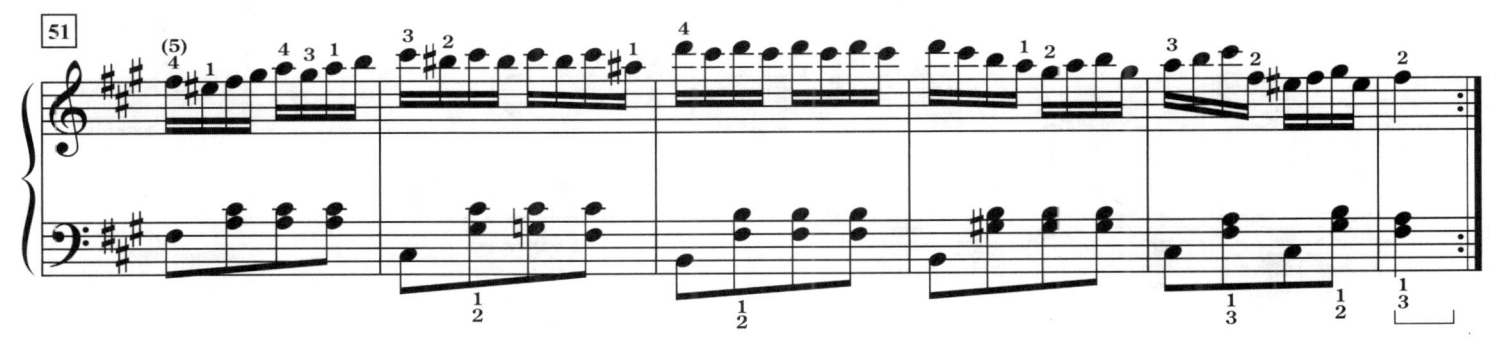

ⓓ Play the LH grace notes and RH arpeggiated chords simultaneously.
Les agréments de la main gauche et les accords arpégés de la main droite se jouent simultanément.
Spiele die Vorschlagsnoten der l.H. gleichzeitig mit den arpeggierten Akkorden der r.H.
Tocar los adornos de la mano izquierda y los acordes arpegiados de la derecha en forma simultánea.

Prelude & Fugue in D Major
from *The Well-Tempered Clavier, Book 1*

Prélude et fugue en ré majeur du *Clavecin bien tempéré, Livre I*
Präludium und Fuge in D-dur, aus *Das Wohltemperierte Klavier, Band 1*
Preludio y fuga en re mayor, del Libro 1 del *Clave bien temperado*

Johann Sebastian Bach (1685–1750)
BWV 850

FUGUE ⓐ

Moderato e maestoso

ⓑ Optional: Double-dotting in the French Overture style can be used in this fugue.
Dans le style de l'ouverture à la française, l'emploi du double point est possible pour cette fugue.
In dieser Fuge kann gemäß dem Stil der Französischen Overtüre Doppelpunktierung verwendet werden.
En la fuga, se pueden usar ritmos con doble puntillo al estilo de la overtura francesa.

ⓑ When the rhythm  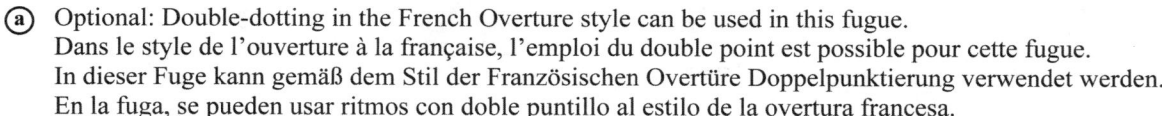 occurs, it is performed as:

Quand on écrit  , on l'éxécute de la façon suivante:

Der Rhythmus  wird wie  ausgeführt.

Cuando aparece este ritmo  , se toca así:

Nocturne in C-sharp Minor

Nocturne en ut dièse mineur
Nocturne in cis-moll
Nocturno en do sostenido menor

Frédéric Chopin (1810–1849)
Op. posthumous

Lento con gran espressione

a Some editions show F-sharp on beats 1 and 3 of the LH.
Quelques éditions indiquent fa dièse au 1er et 3e temps de la main gauche.
L.H. in einigen Ausgaben Fis auf dem 1. und 3. Schlag
Algunas ediciones tienen un fa sostenido en los pulsos 1 y 3 de la mano izquierda.

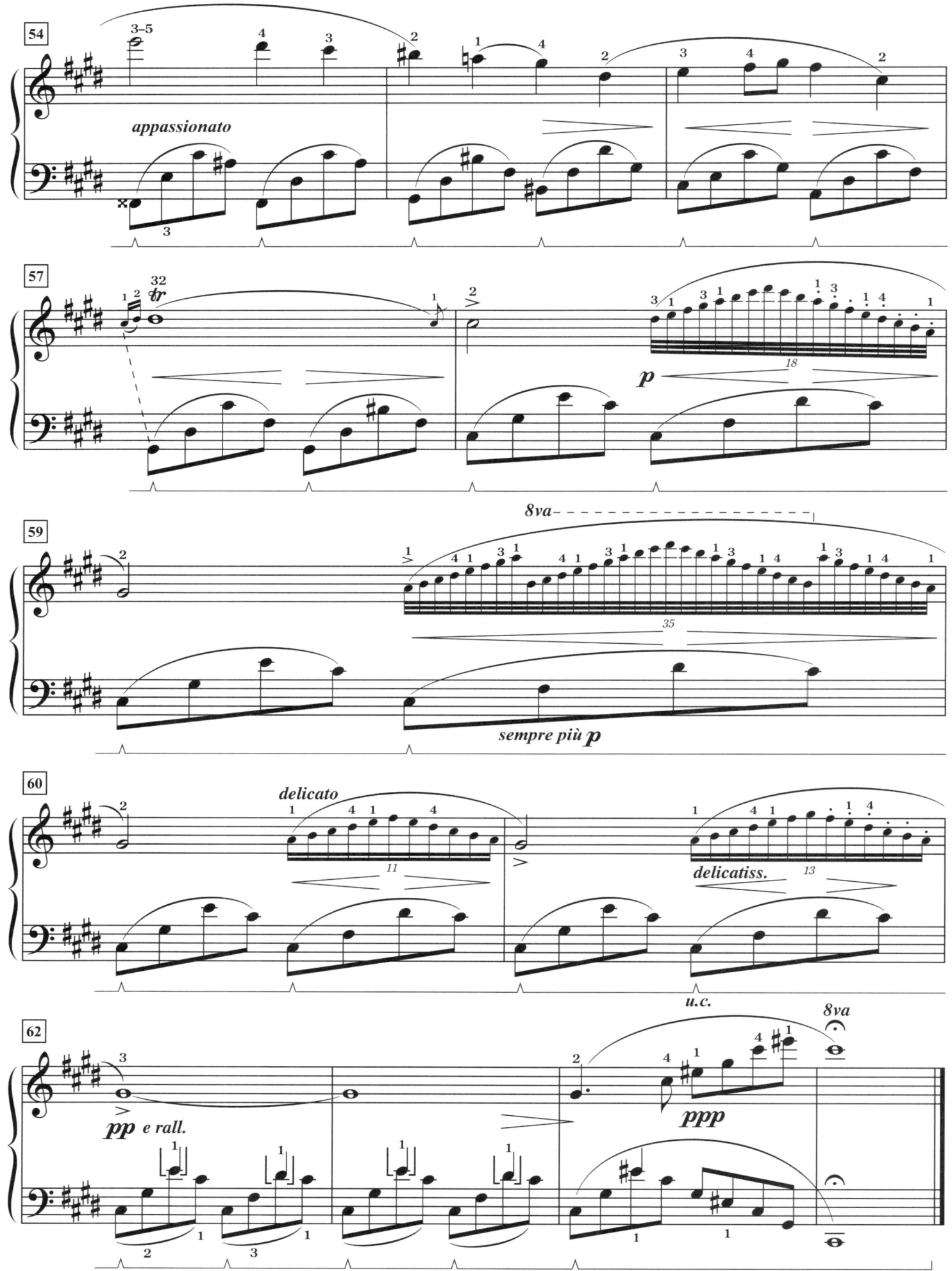

4

The Harmonious Blacksmith
from *Suite No. 5 in E Major*
L'harmonieux forgeron, de la *Suite no 5 en mi majeur*
Der harmonische Grobschmied, aus *Suite Nr. 5 in E-dur*
El herrero armonioso, de la *Suite no 5 en mi mayor*

George F. Handel
(1685–1759)

AIR
Moderato

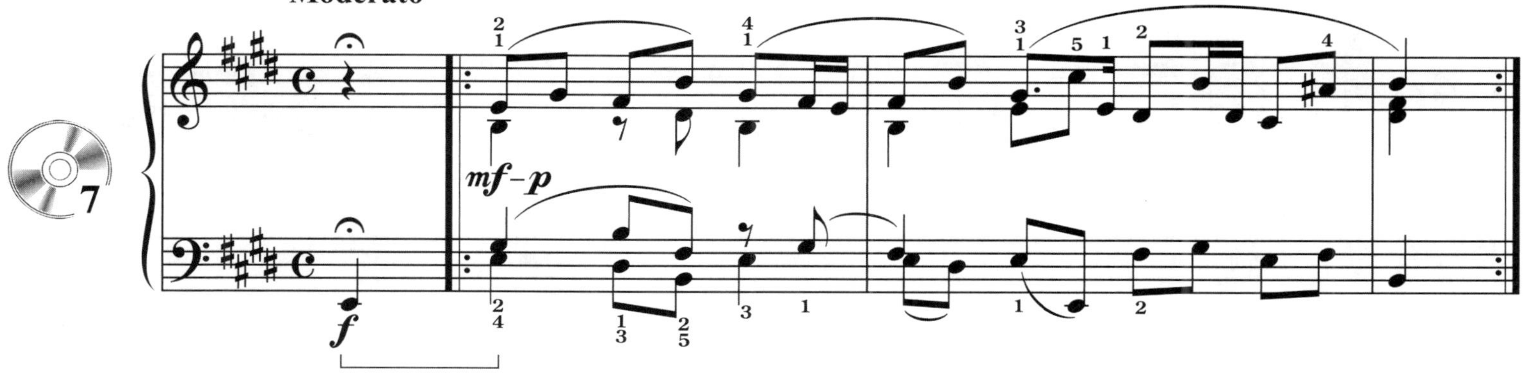

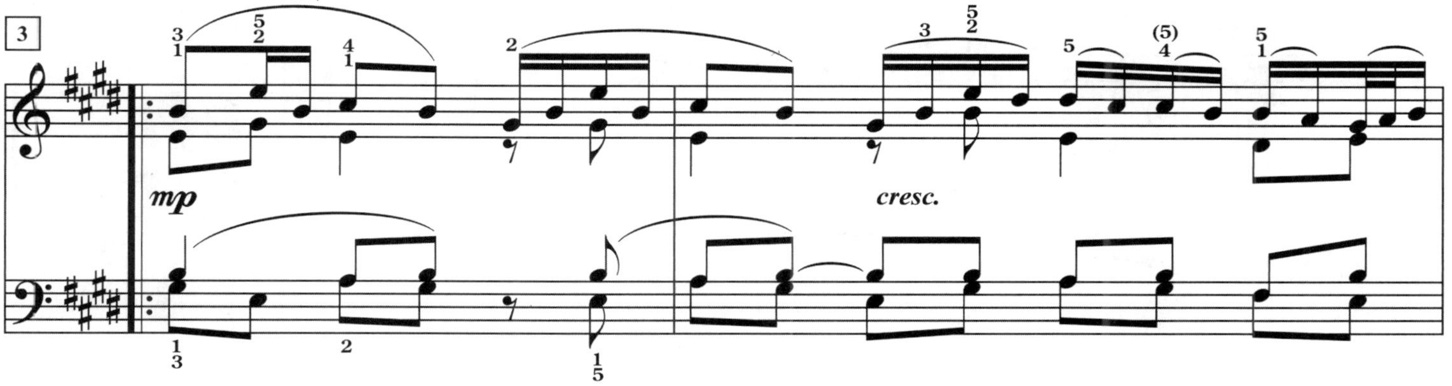

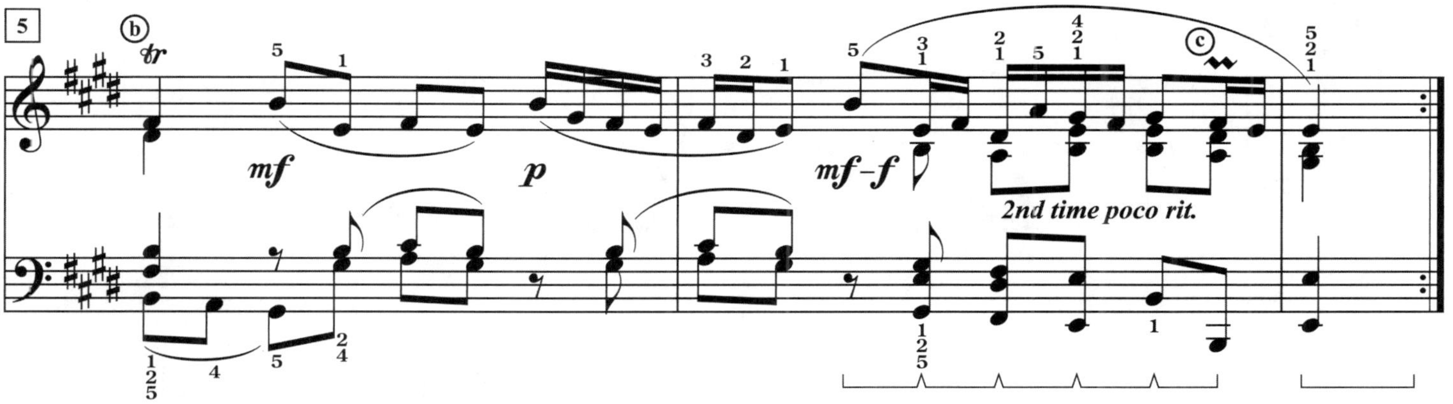

ⓐ The variations in this piece are often called "doubles."
Dans ce morceau, on appelle souvent une variation « un double ».
Die Variationen in diesem Stück werden auch "Doubles" genannt.
Las variaciones de esta pieza muchas veces se llaman "dobles".

ⓑ

ⓒ

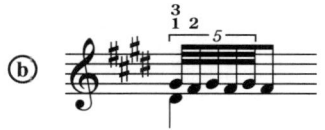

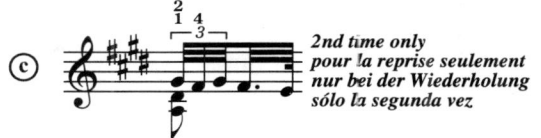

2nd time only
pour la reprise seulement
nur bei der Wiederholung
sólo la segunda vez

La fille aux cheveux de lin
extrait des *Préludes, premier cahier*
The Girl with the Flaxen Hair, from *Préludes, Book 1*
Das Mädchen mit den flachsblonden Haaren, aus *Preludes, Band 1*
La niña de los cabellos de lino, de *Preludios, Libro 1*

Claude Debussy (1862–1918)
L. 117:8

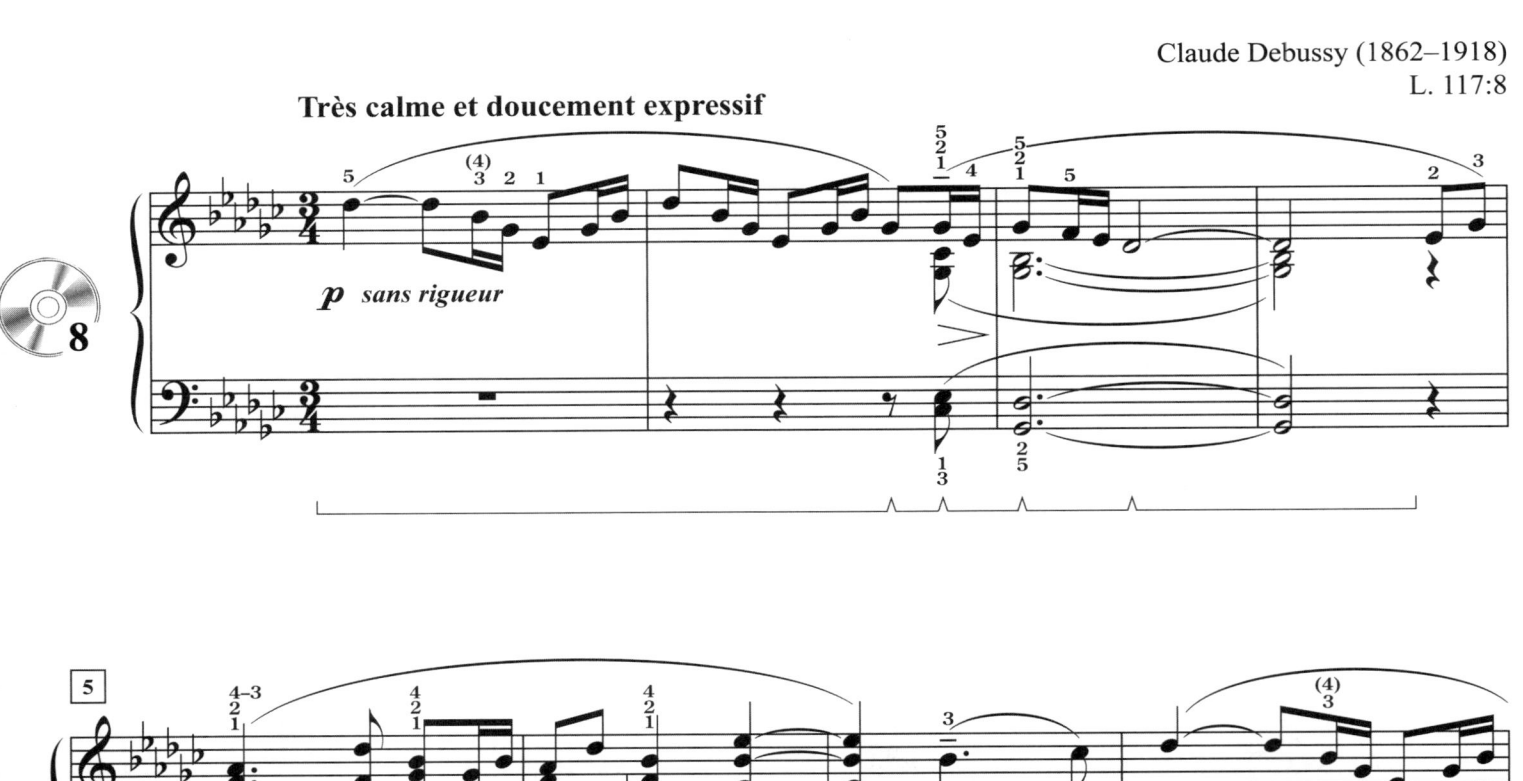

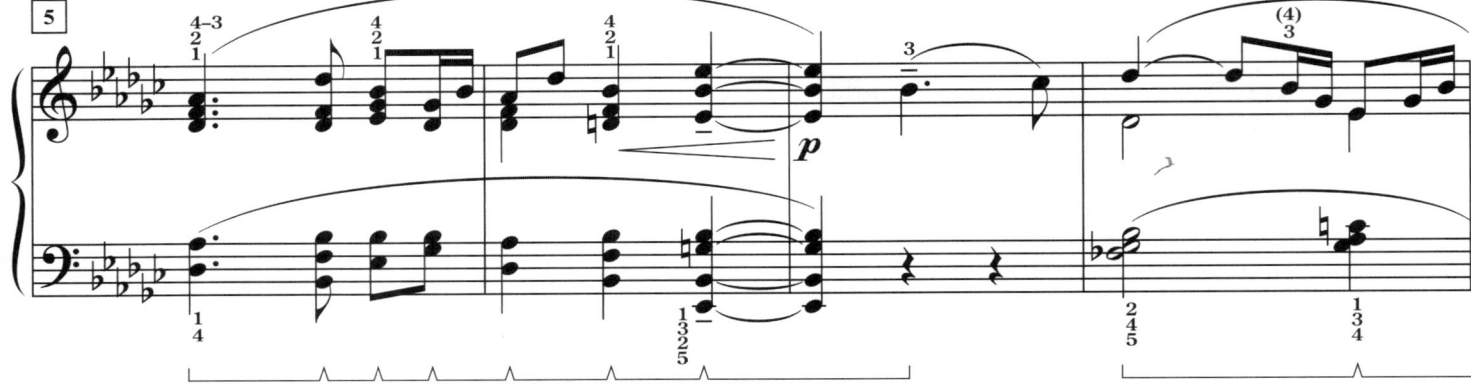

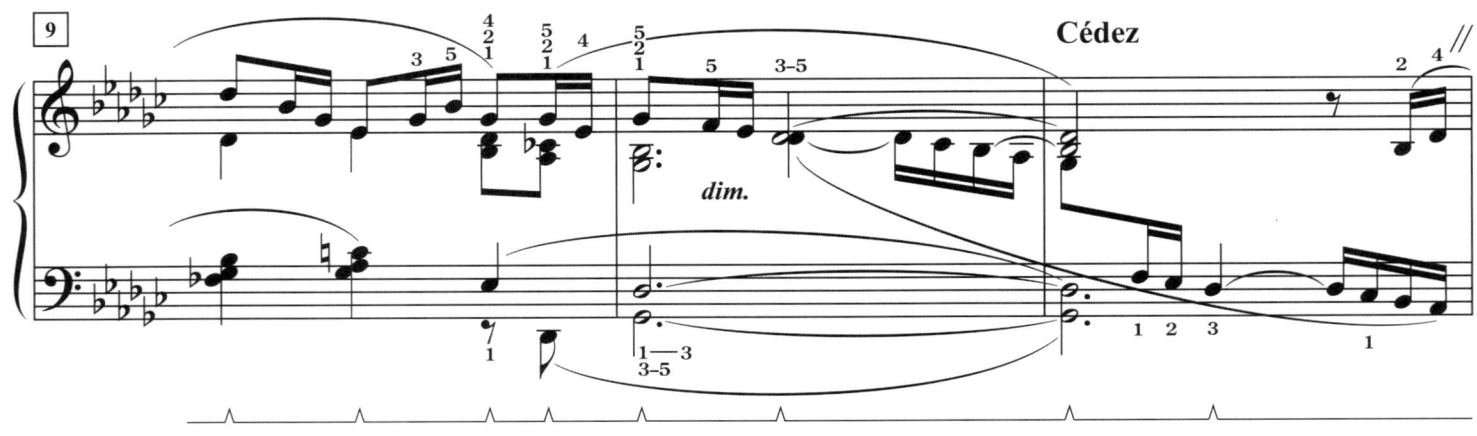

Romanian Folk Dances
Danses populaires roumaines
Rumänische Volkstänze
Danzas folklóricas rumanas

Béla Bartók (1881–1945)
Sz. 56

1. Joc cu Bâtă
(Stick Dance) (Danse du bâton) (Der Tanz mit dem Stabe) (Juego con palos)

2. Brâul

(Waistband Dance) (Danse de la ceinture) (Gürteltanz) (Danza de la faja)

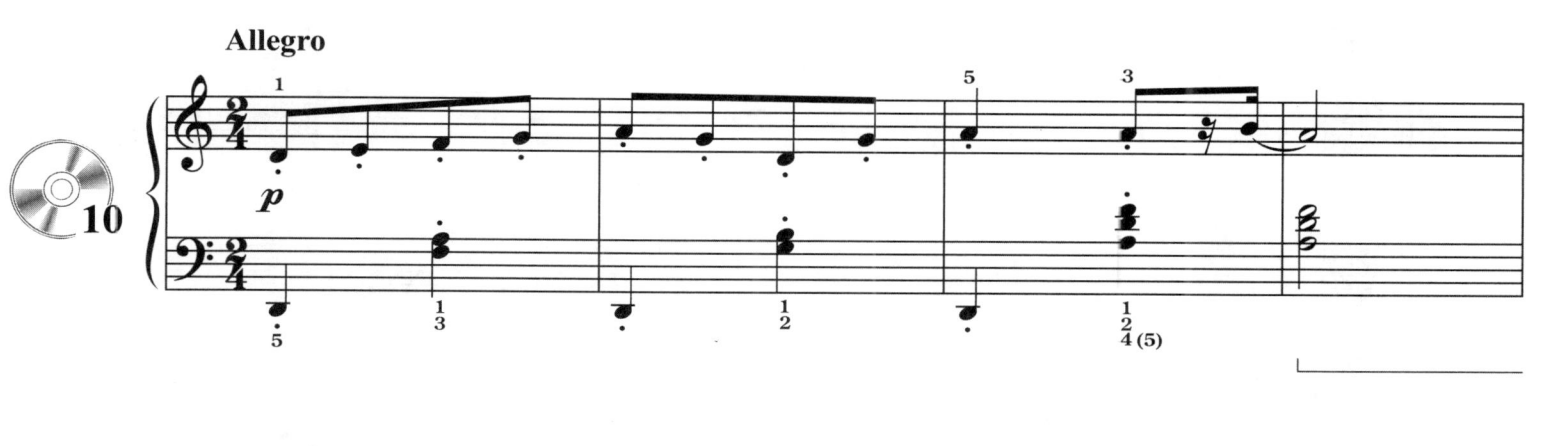

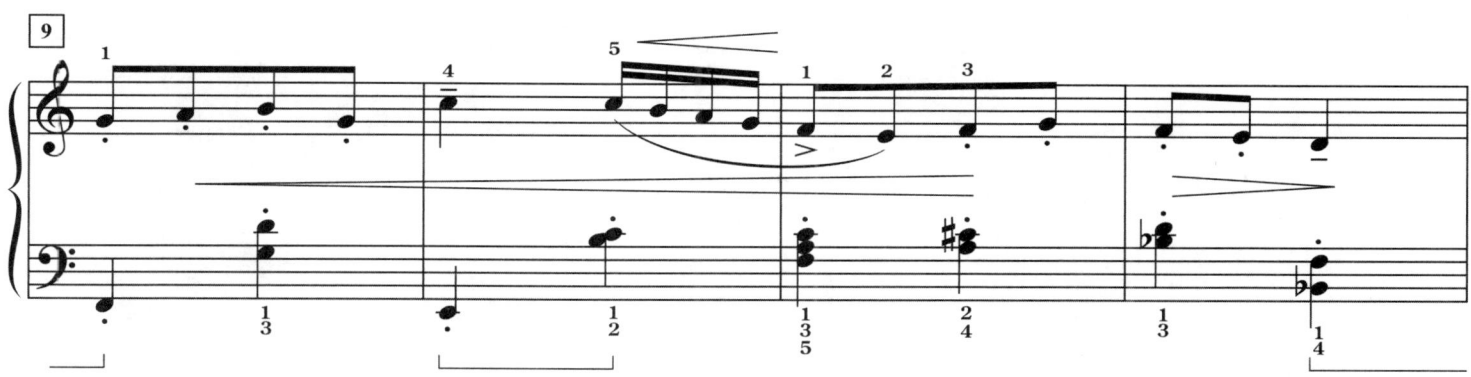
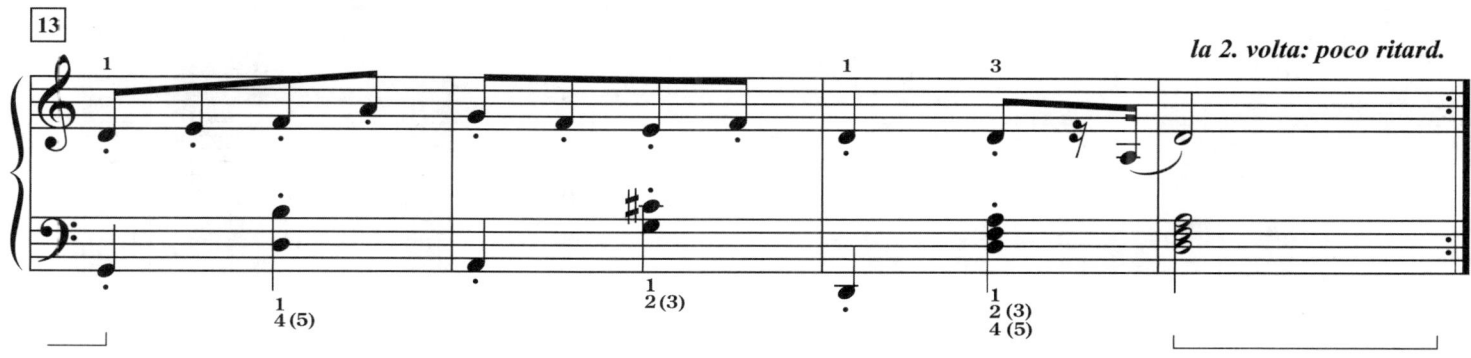

3. Pe loc
(On the Spot) (Trépigneuse) (Der Stampfer) (En un lugar)

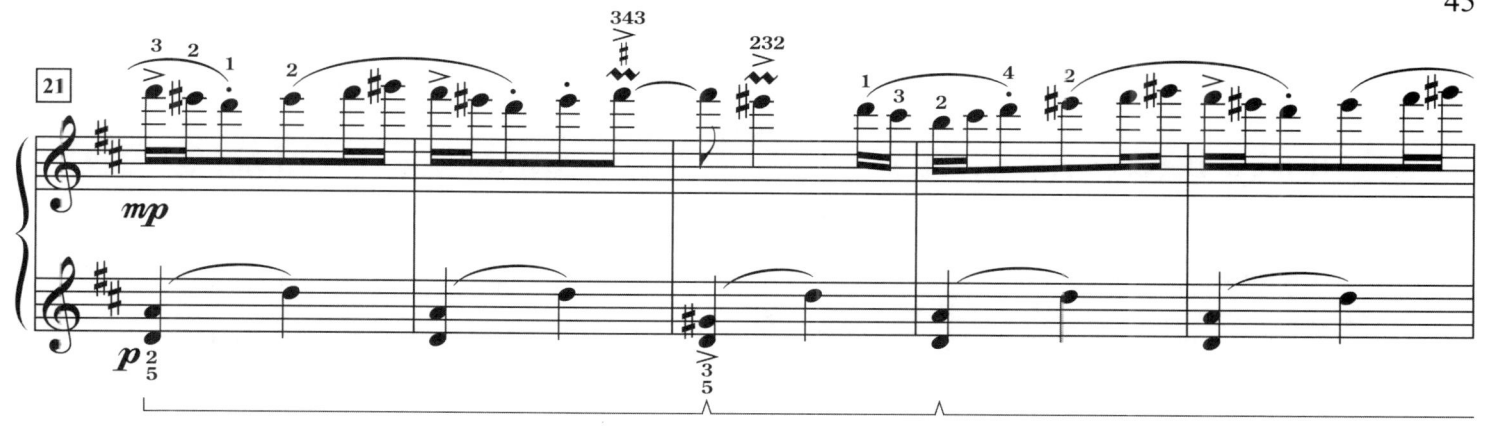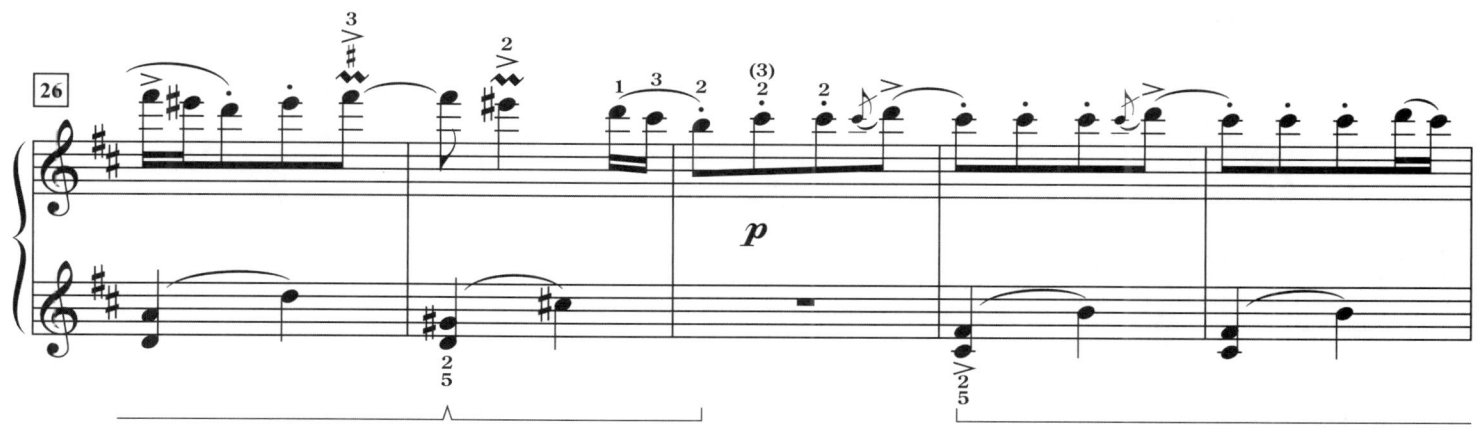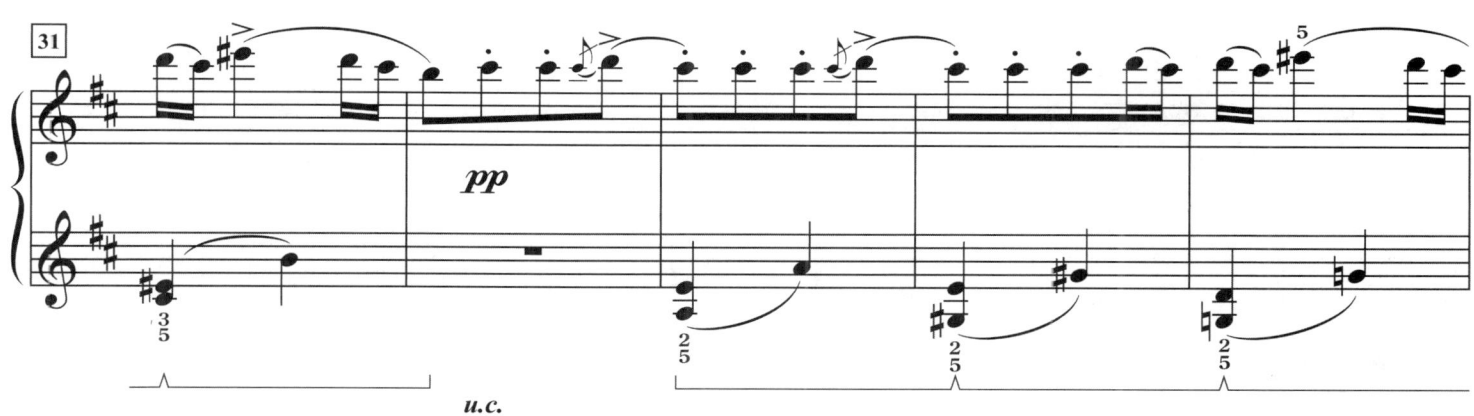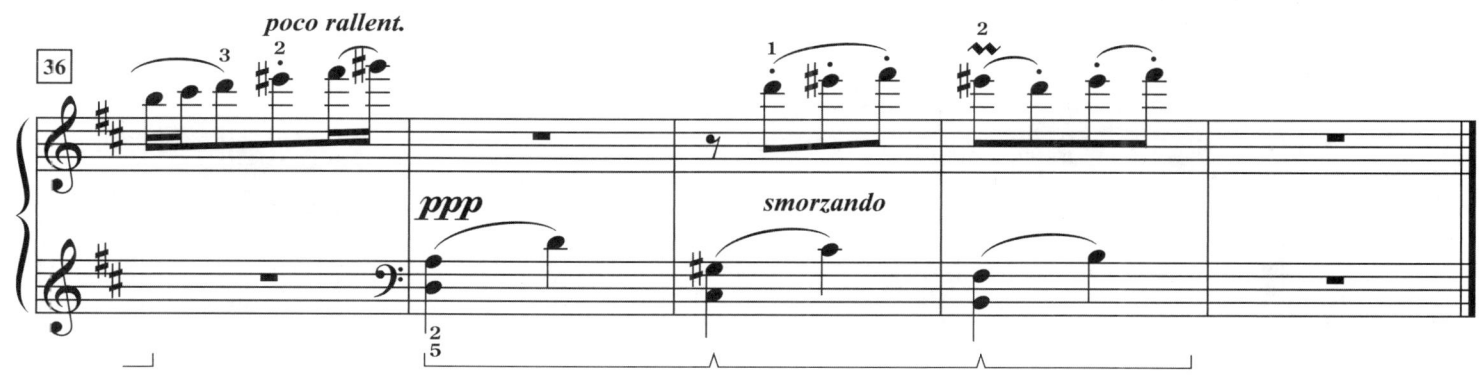

4. Buciumeana

(Dance of Butschum) (Danse de ceux de Bucium) (Tanz aus Butschum) (Danza del cuerno)

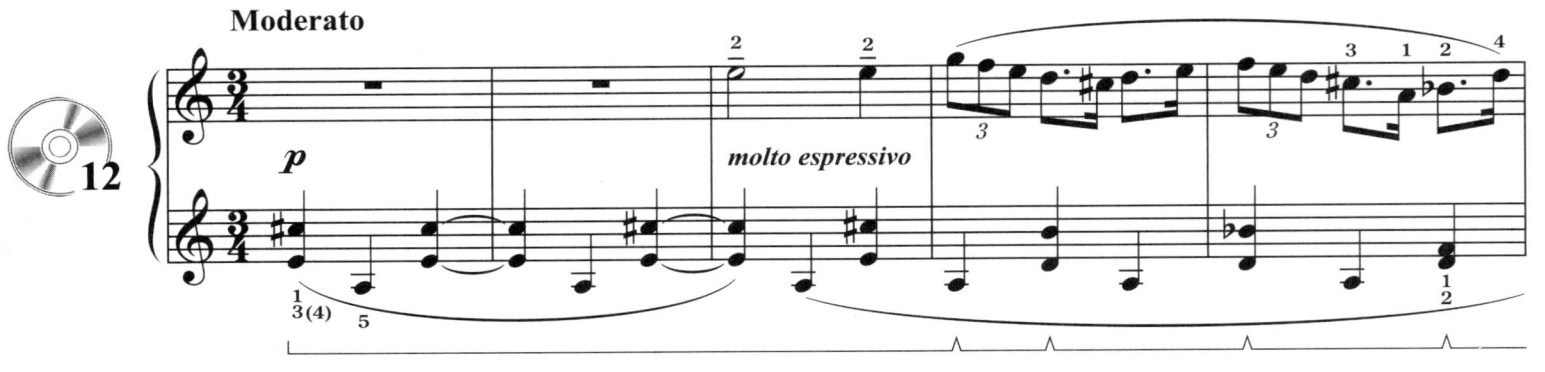
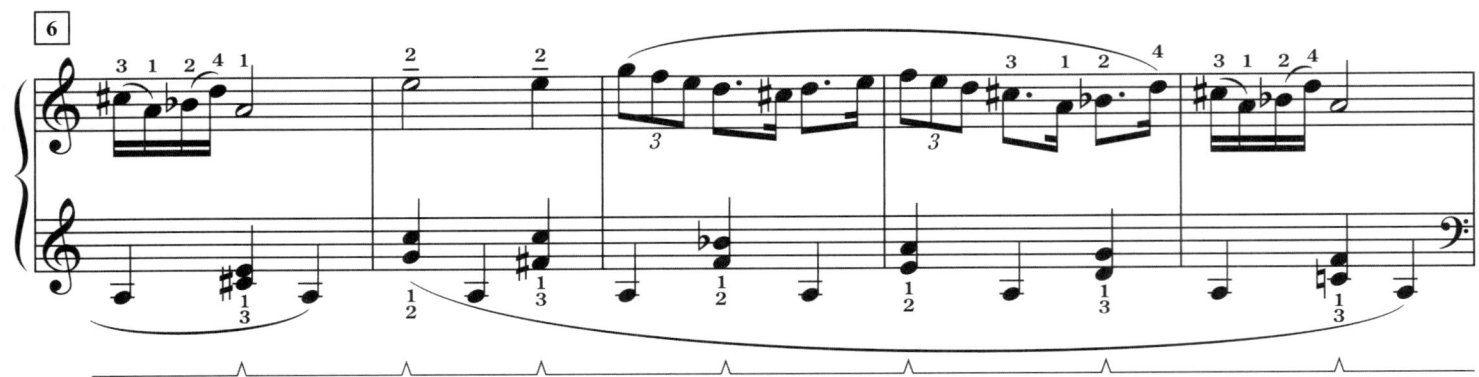
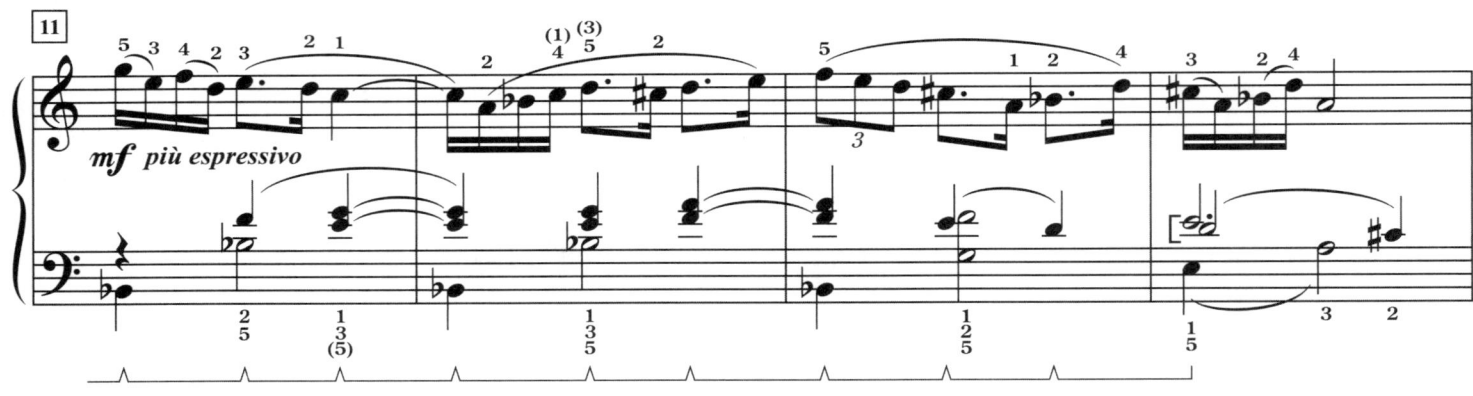
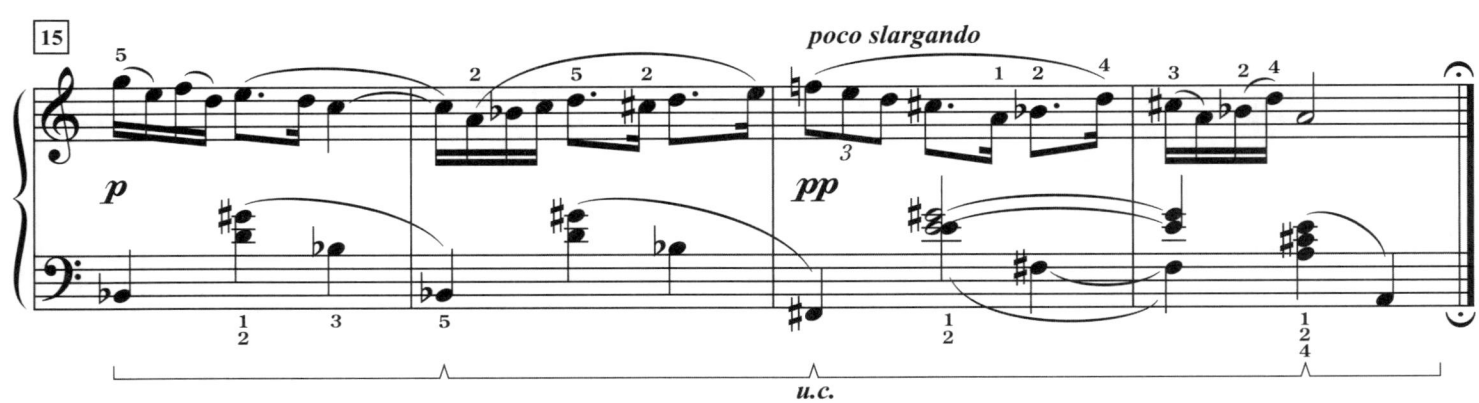

5. Poargă Românească
(Romanian Polka) (Polka roumaine) (Rumänische Polka) (Polka rumana)

6. Măruntelul
(Lively Dance) (Danse précipitée) (Lebhafter Tanz) (Danza animada)